Acknowledgement

The creation of this coffee table book **"Everyday Entrepreneurs,"** has been an inspiring and fulfilling journey. This project would not have been possible without the encouragement, support, and contributions of many individuals.

First and foremost, I extend my deepest gratitude to my mentors for their invaluable guidance and insightful suggestions throughout the process. Their expertise and constructive feedback have greatly shaped the narrative and visual appeal of this book.

A heartfelt thank you goes to the individual sellers, shop owners, and entrepreneurs whose lives and businesses form the heart of this book.

I am also grateful to my parents for their unwavering support, encouragement, and belief in my vision. Their guidance and constant motivation have been a cornerstone of my efforts and have inspired me every step of the way.

Finally, I want to acknowledge my role as the sole photographer for this book. Capturing the essence of India's bazaars and street sellers through my lens has been an incredible journey that I am proud to share with you all.

"Everyday Entrepreneurs " is a labor of love and collaboration, and I am deeply thankful to everyone who has played a part in bringing this vision to life.

Ishaan

Disclaimer

This coffee table book is a creative project designed for informational and educational purposes. The content reflects the author's independent research, interpretation, and artistic perspective on the subject matter. It may not fully represent professional opinions, current industry standards, or real-life scenarios. All information and imagery are based on publicly available sources, historical references, or creative inspiration unless otherwise cited.

The views, interpretations, and conclusions expressed in this book are those of the author(s) and do not necessarily represent the opinions of any institution, organization, or external body. Any resemblance to actual persons, events, or entities is purely coincidental unless explicitly stated.

This coffee table book is not intended as a substitute for professional advice or consultation. Neither the author(s) nor the publisher assume any responsibility for actions or decisions made based on the content provided.

Introduction
The Contribution Of Street Vendors To The Indian Economy

Street vendors are considered an integral part of life in India; from vegetables and fruits to milk, everything that people require in their daily living is available from sellers who trade in the open air. These groups of men and women who quietly work and operate around the clock, winding up their machinery and helping run things smoothly, are the people who make up the rich community we all are a part of. Street vendors offer a wealth of life lessons— from resilience, determination, and courage to being street smart and enterprising. These vendors are perhaps the most adaptive to the ever-evolving market, always working according to the demands of their customers. If a person wants to grasp a range of business and marketing concepts— multitasking, dealing with competition, the importance of presentation and location, and how to keep up with the market trends— observe any street vendor for a few days. They are known by different names across the country, such as hawkers, pheriwalas, and sidewalk traders; they all add to the diverse tapestry of the country.

According to reports, the vast population of street vendors in India exceeds 10 million people. A large part of this street vendor population is economic migrants who come from the country's rural heartland. The Ministry of Urban Development and Poverty Alleviation claims that these 10 million vendors are a paramount part of the Indian economy, contributing to around 50 percent of the country's savings, and surprisingly, 63 percent of the country's GDP comes from these vendors. If we talk about the urban market, these everyday sellers and daily wage workers comprise 4.2 percent of the total employment in the urban economy.

Moving forward, these sellers can easily be considered as micro-entrepreneurs— creating employment not only for themselves but also being an important support for the entire supply chain, ranging from small-scale manufacturers to transporters. In addition to their significant economic contribution, street vendors also serve as cultural ambassadors. This is particularly noticeable when it comes to food vendors, since each meal puts you in touch with the history of Indian cuisine and its regional variations.

Kallan Sweets
DELHI KA FAMOUS
SHARBAT
- E -
MOHBBAT
KALLAN SWEETS. A PURE DESI GHEE PREPARATI
ZAHRA

Bismillah

Saif Tour & Travels
NEW
COOL POINT
COUPON FARE
AVAILABLE
سيف تور تريولس
Saif Tour & Travels

عبد اللّٰه بک ڈپو
Abdullah Book Depot
395- Urdu Market, Gali Mati Mahal, Jama Masjid, Delhi-110006

MANUFACTUR J. WELLERS
NO PASTE
CASH ONLY

Lajawab Handicrafts
WOODEN & STONE HANDICRAFTS
ALL KINDS OF INDIAN HANDICRAFTS
WHITE METAL JEWELLERY
1586, Dariba Kalan, Chandni Chowk, Delhi-110006 (INDIA)
PARAM
Amul

<u>Challenges</u>

Street vendors, who constitute nearly 10% of the market and workforce in the informal sector, are considered the backbone of the economy; however, their everyday lives are marked by systemic challenges. These vendors typically operate in a legal grey zone despite being protected under Article 19(1) and the Street Vendors Act, 2014, which ensures the establishment of vending zones. Many of these vendors report the confiscation of their goods, arbitrary eviction, and financial struggles.

Moreover, these vendors, who spend around 14-18 hours on the streets in hazardous conditions, report chronic respiratory and other health issues. As summer approaches, heatwaves become more frequent, increasing the chances of street vendors experiencing heat strokes and a lack of shaded rest areas.

Street vendors also lack access to basic necessities, such as access to public toilets, forcing them to pay daily at private facilities. According to a report that covered around 15 Indian metropolitan cities, it was found that about 65 percent of the vendors took loans from moneylenders at excessive interest rates ranging from around 120 to 400 percent, making it difficult for them to achieve financial stability and keeping several vendors permanently in debt.

Even though they play an important role in urban economies, there are persistent challenges that street vendors face on an everyday basis, highlighting the urgent need for more inclusive policies, better implementation of existing laws and greater support to ensure that street vendors can work with dignity, security, and access to basic amenities in India's rapidly evolving cities.

RZLARMY

How Can We Help Them?

Street vendors play an indispensable role in India's urban economy by providing affordable goods and services to millions of people, generating employment, and contributing to the vibrancy of city life. However, despite their significance, street vendors face persistent challenges such as legal insecurity, financial instability, and a lack of access to basic amenities like clean water, sanitation, and waste disposal facilities. Many vendors operate without formal recognition, leaving them vulnerable to harassment, eviction, and exploitation.

To address these issues, it is crucial to implement and enforce comprehensive laws that protect the rights of street vendors. The Street Vendors (Protection of Livelihood and Regulation of Street Vending) Act, 2014, is a landmark piece of legislation designed to safeguard vendors' livelihoods and regulate street vending activities. Urban local bodies must take proactive steps to conduct regular surveys to identify and register all street vendors, ensuring that no one is left out. Issuing government-registered ID cards can provide vendors with a sense of security and legitimacy, making it easier for them to access welfare schemes and financial services. Additionally, authorities should design and maintain well-equipped vending zones with adequate access to water, sanitation, and waste management, which would greatly improve vendors' working conditions and public health.

Community organisations and local NGOs have a pivotal role to play in supporting street vendors. They can advocate for vendors' rights, help them understand legal provisions, and provide financial literacy education. Collaborating on training programs that cover digital payments, business management, and adapting to changing markets can empower vendors to grow their businesses sustainably. As responsible citizens, supporting street vendors by choosing to buy from them and participating in local initiatives can create a meaningful impact, helping to build a more inclusive and resilient urban economy.

PARAM

PARAM

HOSIERY & READYMADE GARM

NEW BOOK LAND NEW

Gōkulam
PhonePe
WATER

MOTHER DAIRY
100% MILK ICE CREAM
Pay

The Embassy
KWALITY WALL'S
KWALITY WALL'S

NO ENTRY WITHOUT
FACE MASK

Conclusion

Daily wage labourers and street vendors can rightly be called the unsung heroes of the ever-changing Indian urban landscape - enterprising, resilient, and a part of our daily lives. These micro-entrepreneurs play a crucial role in the informal economy, supporting multiple families and helping to introduce India's tastes and traditions to every corner of the country on an everyday basis.

However, their lives are not easy, as they face persistent legal ambiguities and financial vulnerability, health risks, and the big issue of respect, dignity, and societal recognition. Despite such hurdles and struggles, street vendors have developed the ability to adapt, innovate, and respond to the changing market demands.

As the Indian urban landscape undergoes an evolution, the stories and struggles of every single street vendor serve as a reminder that real progress is best measured by the inclusivity of its public spaces. Supporting street vendors through better policies, infrastructures, and community engagement should be viewed as the responsibility of every citizen and organisation.